Original title:
Saturn's Stand-Up Set

Copyright © 2025 Creative Arts Management OÜ
All rights reserved.

Author: Gideon Barrett
ISBN HARDBACK: 978-1-80567-812-0
ISBN PAPERBACK: 978-1-80567-933-2

Humor Among the Rings

In the shadow of gas, the jokes take flight,
Rings of laughter swirl in the starlit night.
Giant chuckles bounce off moons in a race,
While comets roll their eyes, just keeping pace.

A jester in orbit, with wit that astounds,
Too many punchlines to fit in the rounds.
Each ring a reminder of fun cosmic schemes,
As we giggle aloud at the most outlandish dreams.

The Saturnine Comedian

With a laugh that shimmers, like light on the cold,
The jester's quips sparkle, a sight to behold.
He tells of mishaps with meteors flying,
While alien crowds gather, breathlessly sighing.

His tales of the cosmos, a wild, swirling spree,
Each punchline delivered, brings tears full of glee.
From the depths of the void to the heart of the sun,
In the comedy club, every night is pure fun.

Cosmic Kicks and Quips

Drifting through space, he trips on a star,
"Did you hear about gravity? It takes me too far!"
Spinning in orbit, he does a great twirl,
While laughter erupts, like a cosmic swirl.

With meteoric puns and stellar one-liners,
Each belly-laugh echoes among the diviners.
A galaxy full of jokes, bright as can be,
Creating light-years of pure comedy.

Laughter in the Ether

On a throne made of stardust, he rules the night,
Each laugh in the ether, a contagious delight.
When planets align, the humor takes flight,
As moons orbit round, sharing bliss in their light.

In the quiet of space, the giggles arise,
From the depths of the void to the radiant skies.
With jokes that are timeless, like stars set to shine,
In this cosmic stand-up, we all intertwine.

Orbital Oddities

In the rings of gold and grey,
A joke flew by in a playful way.
"Why did the moon refuse to fight?"
"It couldn't find its own light!"

With planets laughing, all in cheer,
A gas giant jokes, but is hard to hear.
"Why did the comet break up with its date?"
"Too much tail, it couldn't relate!"

Comet's Comedic Odyssey

A comet dashed across the night,
With puns so bright, a pure delight.
"Why don't stars ever get lost?"
"They always know their spacey cost!"

Through the cosmos, the laughter soared,
As asteroids chuckled, never bored.
"What did the nebula say to the sun?"
"Stop being so bright, it's no fun!"

Gravitational Gags

In the warp and weft of cosmic art,
Gravity pulls, but still a heart.
"Why did the black hole fail its test?"
"It couldn't pull in enough jest!"

Around the star, the laughter swirled,
As galaxies twirled in a comical world.
"What did the astronaut lose in space?"
"His sense of humor—what a silly case!"

Jovial Journeys

On a rocket ride with a silly crew,
An alien yells, "I brought snacks too!"
"Why was the rocket feeling low?"
"It couldn't find its lift-off flow!"

Through the cosmos, they sang and joked,
While silly stars danced and choked.
"Why don't satellites ever get cold?"
"Because they're always orbiting gold!"

Universe of Uncommon Laughs

In the cosmos where jokes collide,
Stars giggle, and meteors slide.
Nebulas puff with laughter bright,
As planets spin in pure delight.

A comet winks with a silly grin,
While black holes jest, 'We suck you in!'
Galaxies swirl in a cosmic dance,
Each twinkle's a punchline, given a chance.

Alien guests share quirky tales,
Of space-time follies and interstellar fails.
Satellites chuckle, 'We orbit for fun!'
Creating humor where there's none.

So lift off your spirits, up to the sky,
Join the laughter where stardust flies.
In this universe, so wild and vast,
The best of the jokes are made to last.

Laughter Among the Stars

In the ether where jokes collide,
Planets giggle and comets slide.
Stars twinkle in a cosmic show,
As they trade puns in a stellar glow.

Heightened humor from afar,
Moons chuckle loud, 'You're a star!'
With every quip, a meteor flies,
Witty banter under night skies.

Galactic punchlines float with grace,
Nebulas laugh, oh, what a place!
Laughter echoes across the void,
Space is bright, and dreams enjoyed.

Comedy Over Cosmic Dust

Beyond the worlds where the wild jokes roam,
Laughter drifts as we find our home.
Dusty asteroids cracking wise,
Meteorites throwing punchlines that rise.

Near distant suns, a troupe performs,
Galactic gags in playful forms.
Planets spin in blissful mirth,
While comets sing of their light-hearted birth.

In the spiral arms, a stage is set,
With witty wonders we won't forget.
So gather round, the cosmos shines,
In every giggle, the universe twines.

Cheerful Tales from the Skies

Above the clouds, where the starlight beams,
Giggles bounce, igniting dreams.
Astro-heroes in capes of light,
Crafting tales to delight the night.

Watch the satellites sharing jokes,
Spinning tales that tickle folks.
Each constellation plays its part,
With a punchline that's straight from the heart.

Through the void, the laughter soars,
As galaxies spin and friendship pours.
Every twinkling is a smile's embrace,
In the cosmic theater, we find our place.

An Astral Chuckle

In the orbit of mirth, the comets tease,
While black holes giggle with effortless ease.
Galaxies twist in joyous surprise,
As they dance to the rhythm of comical skies.

Shooting stars flash with a wink and a grin,
Whispering secrets of laughter within.
Jokes that travel at light-speed so fast,
Bringing joy from the future and past.

Through the cosmic arena, they play a show,
As starry-eyed beings let their humor flow.
In this endless expanse, we're never alone,
For laughter among the heavens is truly our own.

The Void's Vaudeville

In the depths of space, I take my stage,
With comets lined up, they cheer and gage.
Planets drop in for a chuckle or two,
Stars shining bright with the laughs that ensue.

A black hole's punchline, it draws you near,
It swallows the jokes, but we persevere.
Galaxies swirling in a cosmic whirl,
They spit out the puns with a twirl and a twirl.

My companion, the moon, does a dance quite absurd,
He wobbles and jiggles, it's truly unheard.
Ringed giants snicker, as they watch with disbelief,
While asteroids tumble, chasing comic relief.

So let's toast to the jokes that light up the night,
In the theater of stars, we'll laugh till it's bright.
In the vacuum of silence, our giggles will play,
In the void of vaudeville, we live for today.

Laughter's Lightyears Away

A quasar bursts forth with a cosmic jest,
Those lightyears away find it hard to digest.
Einstein chuckles at space-time's strange bends,
As gravity pulls, but humor transcends.

Venus is blushing, the sun's in a grin,
While planets spin round, let the laughter begin.
Meteor showers drop punchlines with flair,
And the echoes of giggles dance through the air.

Through the Milky Way, the jokes float along,
With every new quip, the universe's song.
So if you feel distant, just look to the skies,
Comedy travels on light-speed replies.

As I sit in my ship, with my crew made of stars,
We share all the humor as we zoom past the Mars.
In galaxies far, where the funny grows gray,
It warms up my heart, laughter's lightyears away.

Jovian Jestbook

Jupiter laughs with a booming delight,
Moons gather 'round for a comedy night.
The storms swirl in rhythm, a giggle, a roar,
As orbits align for an encore galore.

I jot down the jests in my Jovian tome,
With wild cosmic tales from this gaseous home.
The rings of dust swirl like confetti at play,
While giants above hold a mirthful ballet.

The oxygen party gets lively and bright,
With hydrogen jokes that just take off in flight.
Spectacular punchlines bounce off every cloud,
While the laughter erupts, growing louder and loud.

So here's to the whispers from thick atmospheres,
Where humor ignites amidst cosmic frontiers.
In the pages of space, let the funny unwind,
For in this vast jestbook, true comedy's blind.

Gravitational Giggles

Pull on my heartstrings, the gravity's fun,
With a weighty old humor from the planet run.
Each pull of the joke brings us closer to cheer,
In this cosmic ballet, absurdities steer.

Asteroids bounce like kids on the floor,
With laughter that echoes, who could want more?
Satellites giggle as they float by and sway,
In a spiral of humor, we dance and we play.

The comedy cracks like meteoroid breaks,
In the orbit of jokes, we're all great at fakes.
We tumble through space, unbound by the laws,
Finding joy in the chaos, and laughter's applause.

Underneath the stars, we share silly dreams,
With gravitational pulls, it's not what it seems.
So raise up your voices, let the fun be like wine,
In this universe vast, where the giggles align.

The Humor of the Heliosphere

In the void where planets spin,
Jokes are told to keep us grinnin'.
Asteroids chuckle in the night,
While comets race, what a sight!

Witty stars twinkle and glare,
Spreading laughter through the air.
On meteors, pranks take flight,
In the cosmos, humor ignites.

Galactic echoes of delight,
Bounce off orbits, what a fright!
Black holes hide their punchlines tight,
Waiting for their grand debut night.

With every quasar's bright beam,
Laughter dances in a dream.
In this sphere of cosmic jest,
Life's too short, so let's invest!

Laughter Beyond the Light Years

Jupiter's storms play a tune,
While Mercury hums 'round the moon.
From Neptune's depths, a joke arises,
Each solar wave, a surprise!

In the vacuum, giggles swell,
Mars cracked a pun, can't you tell?
Time flies fast, but laughter lingers,
Across the cosmos, shared fingers.

Light years stretch, but humor binds,
Witty rhymes in all our minds.
In the dark, we find the glow,
Of cosmic tales that steal the show.

Beyond our reach, yet so near,
Galactic giggles, crystal clear.
Space-time bends with each new jest,
Join the laughter, it's the best!

Stardust Stand-Up

Galaxies twirl, a dizzy dance,
Swirling humor at every chance.
Nebulae burst with comedic flair,
Astrophysics? More like a dare!

Meteorites crash with fun-filled glee,
Telling tales of what could not be.
Space dust shuffles in cosmic rhyme,
Creating chuckles that stand the time.

Eclipses wink, pulling pranks on sight,
While astronauts giggle at their flight.
Comedies bloom in the Milky Way,
Stars share laughter on their grand stay.

In this universe, full of cheer,
Sharing jokes is why we're here.
So let's raise a toast to the night,
For in stardust, we find delight!

The Rings of Revelry

Around the giant, circles play,
Rings of laughter brighten the fray.
Satellites spin with jokes to share,
A cosmic party, come unaware!

Ice and rock in a playful whirl,
Each rotation brings a swirl.
Laughter arcs in the vacuum wide,
As space fills up with joy and pride.

Io tells tales of misfit moons,
While echoes dance to laughing tunes.
Gravity pulls, but humor soars,
In this realm, no one bores.

With each band of light that gleams,
We stitch our bonds through shared dreams.
The rings unite us in this jest,
In cosmic joy, we find our best!

Celestial Satire Spectacle

In the void where planets spin,
A jester's grin could draw you in.
With comedic charm so bright,
Stars chuckle in the cosmic night.

Asteroids drop punchlines rare,
While moons roll with uproarious flair.
A comet's tail sways in delight,
As laughter echoes through the night.

Nebulas swirl in vibrant hues,
Crafting jokes like cosmic blues.
Galaxies twist in glee and jest,
Telling tales of space's best.

Gravity pulls on your sides,
While space-time wobbles in wild rides.
Celestial bodies break the mold,
In a comedy show that's pure gold.

The Cosmic Stage of Comedy

In the expanse where humor reigns,
Starry smiles erase all pains.
Pulsars pulse with witty lines,
While black holes hide comedic signs.

Meteor showers bring the fun,
As starlight dances, one by one.
Quasars beam a laugh or two,
In the cosmic show, who knew?

Astrologers laugh at their fate,
Stargazers giggle, it's never late.
Planets punt the puns with flair,
Galaxy jokes float through the air.

On this stage above the strife,
Galactic giggles breathe new life.
The universe, a grand old jest,
In the cosmos, laughter's the best.

Celestial Comedy

Within the stars, a funny tale,
Satellites spin like a comedy trail.
Supernovae burst with surprise,
Jokes carried on the cosmic skies.

Radiant rays of humor gleam,
Galactic giggles fuel the dream.
Laughter sparkles among the stars,
As planets share their silly scars.

A cosmic dance of care-free jest,
Holding all the universe's best.
In a celestial, comedic spree,
Even the moons join in with glee.

Across the night, we share our jokes,
Asteroids join with silly pokes.
In every chuckle, darkness fades,
As laughter fills the cosmic glades.

Rings of Laughter

Around the giant, rings of fun,
Each laugh a spark, a joy to run.
Witty quips float side by side,
In the orbits where humor abides.

With echoes ringing through the void,
Every pithy jest is deployed.
Twinkling stars dance with delight,
In the grip of cosmic light.

Planets play their parts so well,
Telling tales of humor to tell.
Rings of laughter twist and swirl,
In this universe, joy's the pearl.

So strap in tight for the cosmic ride,
As laughter ignites the stellar tide.
In the grandeur of the night's embrace,
Everyone shares in this funny space.

Orbital Observations

Rings of dust and ice so bright,
Whirling round in cosmic light.
They caught a comet's wild dance,
A ball of gas in a cosmic trance.

Moons are laughing, playing pranks,
Twirling 'round in starlit banks.
One says, "Where's my ice cream sun?"
The other shouts, "You ate the fun!"

Nebulas chuckle in dusty pools,
While robots rust and act like fools.
A cosmic giggle, a cosmic cheer,
Echoes softly from a distant sphere.

In this vast and goofy space,
Every planet has its place.
With every quirk and every jest,
The universe hosts the funniest fest.

Jovian Jokes

Under the clouds of stormy skies,
A giant laughs, much to our surprise.
"Why did the moon go to school?"
"To get a little brighter, you fool!"

With swirling winds and playful gales,
This behemoth tells the best of tales.
"Why's my girlfriend got a bad hair day?"
"She's just trying to wear that Milky Way!"

Its moons roll eyes in cosmic jest,
While meteors slate the universe's best.
Chortling comets cut their path,
Leaving behind a playful laugh.

Jupiter twirls in a jolly spin,
As each joke echoes from within.
A kingdom of laughter, bright and bold,
In its majestic arms, stories unfold.

The Clown of the Cosmos

In a costume sewn from starlight threads,
Pranks and giggles light up the spreads.
Planets wobble and blush in delight,
While comets dance, skipping through the night.

With a space hat full of silly dreams,
This cosmic fool plots grander schemes.
"Why's the asteroid always on its own?"
"Because it can't find a friend it's known!"

Floating far in the galactic bazaar,
Jokes tumble down like a shooting star.
"Why did the star refuse to shine?"
"Too busy baking its celestial pie!"

A laugh that rumbles through the void,
Even black holes can't be annoyed.
The joker brings joy across the sky,
In the universe's arms, we laugh and fly!

Asteroids and Anecdotes

Bouncing rocks with stories to tell,
Like comedians, they cast their spell.
"Why did the asteroid miss the show?"
"It lost its orbit and couldn't go!"

Drifting through the galactic hall,
Each a character, each a call.
"Why don't asteroids ever get lost?"
"They just follow the stars, at no cost!"

With chuckles rolling through the night,
Each one shining, bold and bright.
"Why did the moon break up with the sun?"
"Too hot to handle, just not fun!"

An orbit packed with humor and glee,
Their anecdotes float so carefree.
In a cosmos where laughter reigns,
Even silence giggles and entertains.

Humor in the Heavens

In the night sky, jokes collide,
Stars chuckle softly, can't hide.
Galaxies twist, they dance and play,
Making light of each black hole's sway.

Asteroids hurl witty comets glee,
Meteor showers, a slapstick spree.
Planets giggle in orbits round,
Echoes of laughter, a cosmic sound.

Constellations form a merry band,
Drawing laughter across the land.
Twinkling lights in a comic show,
Echoing jokes that only they know.

In the vast dark where humor's bright,
Even the moon gets in on the light.
With every wink, a joke is told,
In the fabric of space, joy unfolds.

The Prankster Planet

Oh, the planet with a curious grin,
Tossing pranks like confetti within.
A hop, a skip, a laugh out loud,
Jokester vibes wrap the night like a shroud.

With rings that jingle, they flick and twirl,
Each twist of fate causes laughter to whirl.
A cosmic whoopee cushion, oh what a sight,
It rumbles and giggles deep into the night.

Its moons are a band of merry jesters,
Performing tricks, true cosmic testers.
Planetary gags, they never fall flat,
They send the stars rolling, imagine that!

Amongst the cosmos, there's always some fun,
As shadows of laughter dance on the run.
When the cosmos celebrates with a twinkling wink,
Even the sternest of folks can't help but think.

Rings of Wit

Circling bright with a humorous twist,
Each ring spins tales that none can resist.
A swirl of giggles, a sparkle of cheer,
Each little laugh brings the heavens near.

Spinning gags in a cosmic array,
Galactic banter that lightens the day.
With every rotation, a new punchline found,
In this merry dance of joy, we're all bound.

With every loop, a chuckle in tow,
And wisecracks that outshine the stars' glow.
These rings cascade with humor so bright,
Making the cosmos a jubilant sight.

Orbiting laughter, filled with delight,
Drawing smiles from the dark of the night.
In the embrace of the universe grand,
Wit gathers 'round, forever in hand.

Laughter in the Dark

In the abyss, where shadows reside,
A chuckle erupts, like the cosmic tide.
Stars come alive, sharing fun tales,
Each glowing dot, where joy prevails.

Nebulas burst with colors so bright,
Whispering jokes in the velvet night.
Cosmic clowns in a stellar parade,
Making each moment a memory made.

From black holes to quasars, laughter is sown,
In silence of darkness, humor has grown.
Echoes resound with each playful spark,
The universe smiles, lighting the dark.

In the vastness, joy finds its place,
Crafting delusions, both silly and ace.
With every heartbeat of cosmic delight,
Laughter unfolds in the starry night.

Humor Beyond the Rings

In the cosmos far and wide,
A planet brushed with a grin,
Its rings twinkle like stardust dreams,
Whispering jokes on a whim.

Jupiter laughs at the bloopers,
While Mars cracks a witty line,
With meteors falling like punchlines,
The humor soars through the spine.

Uranus winks with a clever twist,
As comets glide with a jest,
Alien audiences giggle and cheer,
In this space of absolute jest.

Even black holes can chuckle,
As they swallow up a whole beam,
For in this galactic funhouse,
Laughter reigns like a dream.

Light-Year Laughs

Far beyond where the cosmos gleam,
A star tells a joke so bright,
With quarks that dance in delight,
As quasars flicker through the night.

Light-years carry a chuckle too,
Neutrinos giggle with glee,
As black holes swirl with a wink,
In this space comedy spree.

Gravity jokes pull us closer,
While meteors shower in cheer,
The universe feels light and free,
In a laugh-filled atmosphere.

Cosmic rays spark joy unbound,
With every orbit and spin.
In this stellar gag reel,
The funniest tales begin.

Asteroid Anecdotes

Asteroids float with tales untold,
Chugging along like a bus,
Their bumps and bruises tell of laughs,
While whizzing past with no fuss.

One claims it tripped on a comet's tail,
Another said it just danced,
With space dust flying everywhere,
In this galactic, merry trance.

The belt of humor spins and twirls,
As fragments joke in delight,
With laughter echoing through the void,
In the peaceful, starry night.

As they dodge the sun's bright glare,
These rocks of joy collide and play,
Creating laughter like shooting stars,
Lighting up the Milky Way.

Cosmic Clowning

In the circus of the cosmos,
The stars play tricks on the moon,
With planets juggling their orbits,
And sunbeams dancing to a tune.

A comet slips on a starlit stage,
Bringing laughter from afar,
While galaxies spin their colorful wilds,
In this cosmic, crazy bazaar.

Every alien has a punchline,
With jokes that resonate right,
As they gather for a nebula show,
Under the vibrant starlit light.

The universe bursts with laughter's flair,
As laughter echoes through the void,
For in this grand comedic space,
Every moment is a laugh enjoyed.

Voices of the Asteroids

In the belt where rocks collide,
A pebble joked, 'You can't divide!'
I told him, 'You're just a hunk of stone,
Your punchlines land with a dull groan.'

A wanderer from a distant space,
Said, 'I'll make a star laugh in its place!'
But tumbling through, he lost his track,
Now he's the joke we can't take back.

A satellite with flair and might,
Said, 'I shine so bright, I'm pure delight!'
Yet when he slipped on cosmic dust,
His glow turned into rusty rust.

The comets zoom past with speed and grace,
But look! They've got a silly face!
They dance and twirl through the void so vast,
In this asteroid belt, a comic blast!

Humor in the Orbit

Around the sun, they spin and jest,
'Why did the planet take a rest?'
It rolled and said with a playful tone,
'I need my space, I feel alone!'

The moons above in a silly spin,
Chased each other, all for the win.
'Catch me if you can!' they squealed with glee,
But tripped on rings – oh, what a spree!

'Your orbit's off!' shouted from afar,
A tiny asteroid with a broken star.
He laughed until he could not stand,
'This cosmic comedy is totally grand!'

A rocket passed by with a loud honk,
'The universe is no place to donk!'
But just as it sped through the star-lit expanse,
It missed the black hole – oh, what a chance!

Cosmic Snickers

In a universe where laughter swells,
A planetoid recounted tales it tells.
'I tripped on a meteor, what a shock!'
And sent those around into fits of mock.

Nearby, a comet with a wink and a grin,
Said, 'Why so serious? Let the fun begin!'
As it zoomed through space, it flashed a bright light,
Leaving behind a trail of delightful fright.

A space dust bunny waved from a loop,
'Join my comedy club, gather the troupe!'
They joked and jived in the chilly breeze,
As planets rolled by with giggles and wheeze.

The galaxies twinkled, sharing a laugh,
While stars offered tips in their gleaming path.
In this cosmic dance where humor ignites,
Each celestial body, a source of delights!

Jovian Chronicles of Comedic Chaos

On Jupiter's storms where laughter roars,
A giant called out, 'Who ordered more chores?'
'Not me!' squeaked a moon, hemmed in tight,
'This household is wild, and the sun's too bright!'

A vortex spun with a comical flair,
'Twist and turn like you just don't care!'
While clouds gossiped, swirling in jest,
They shared tales of cosmic unrest.

A comet dashed in with a sparkling tail,
'This place is nuts! I'm off the scale!'
But as he zipped past, he started to stall,
And crashed into humor, the best of them all!

With each gas giant joke, the universe shakes,
As time bends and ripples, and chaos awakes.
In Jovian realms, with laughter so bold,
These chronicles shine with stories retold!

Hilarity from the Heavens

In the sky a joke was spun,
Where stars and comets like to run.
Planets chuckle, asteroids wink,
In cosmic humor, we all sink.

Nebulas weave tales so bright,
Of grand old black holes, what a sight!
Galactic gags and playful swings,
A laugh dance through the universe brings.

Cosmic jest, a swirling spree,
While moons all shake in absolute glee.
With each tick of a starlit clock,
The cosmos plays a timeless stock.

So lift your gaze to the night sky,
Where laughter echoes and jokes fly high.
Join the frolic, the joy in the fray,
As the heavens keep humor at bay.

Eclipsed by Laughter

When shadows play a funny game,
And laughter dances without shame.
A solar giggle, a stellar grin,
Where twilight meets the night's din.

Eclipsed by warmth, the stars shine bright,
Moon's punchlines keep the night light.
Black holes roar with their cosmic puns,
And komets burst like silly runs.

Jokes in the void, oh such delight,
With every pause, the darkness fights.
Yet laughter bubbles, no end in sight,
As galaxies twirl in pure delight.

So spin a tale with cosmic cheer,
For each bright twinkle, lend an ear.
In the universe, a jest persists,
With each new dawn, the funny twists.

The Merry Moons

Round and round the laughter flows,
While merry moons strike funny poses.
In a cosmic dance, they swing and twirl,
With giggles echoing through the whirl.

Craters hum with cheerful tunes,
While silver beams spark debate with swoons.
Each phase brings jokes that flip and flop,
As moons in unison swap each prop.

With every cycle, they perform anew,
Touching stardust and dreams so true.
Their laughter fills the cosmic air,
In warm embrace, we all just share.

So gather close, let humor reign,
With merry moons, we banish pain.
In the laughter of the night's embrace,
We find joy in a starry grace.

Rings of Raucous Revelry

Around the giant, a ringed delight,
Where laughs erupt with all their might.
Each twinkle spins a tale so grand,
In the cosmic circus, hand in hand.

With every orbit, the giggles soar,
As rings extend their playful score.
Asteroids clink like glasses in cheer,
While comets dash, angels appear.

In the swirling dance of light and shade,
Laughter cascades, never to fade.
Galactic jesters leap with pride,
In raucous revels, they will bide.

So join the fun in this cosmic spree,
Where humor flows like rivers of glee.
Around the giant, let laughter reign,
In the great expanse, joy is our gain.

Laughing Through the Cosmos

In the vastness where stars play,
Planets spin in a funny way.
Jupiter jokes with a roar,
While asteroids dance across the floor.

Neptune giggles, his rings so grand,
Uranus winks, taking a stand.
Galaxies swirl in laughter bright,
Even black holes smile in the night.

A meteor twirls with a grin,
Shooting by, it can't help but spin.
Quasars beam with cosmic cheer,
While comets dance like they have no fear.

So join in the laughter, take your seat,
In this celestial show, oh so neat.
With humor soaring through the skies,
The universe chuckles, oh what a surprise!

Celestial Stand-Up

The sun cracked a joke, bright and bold,
While moons chuckled softly, stories retold.
Mars snickered, the punchline was clear,
In the comedy club, the stars all cheer.

Venus with her charm, made hearts go 'whoop',
As Saturn spun tales in a swirling hoop.
Earth chimed in with a witty remark,
Creating humorous sparks in the dark.

In the lounge of the universe, jokes abound,
Laughter echoing, a joyous sound.
With each witty quip, gravity bends,
All the cosmos rolling as the fun never ends.

So raise a toast to the cosmic spree,
Where laughter's the key to joy and glee.
With the stars as our audience, play we must,
In this celestial stage, in laughter we trust!

Witty Worlds Collide

Galaxies clash with a comedic sight,
Billing and cooing, what a delight.
Planets throw quips, bright shooting stars,
Tickling the void of the universe's bars.

Black holes joke about the weight of it all,
While Saturn's rings twirl in a cosmic ball.
Alien laughter, an echo so sweet,
As worlds collide in a jolly beat.

Nebulas giggle, with colors that pop,
Comedians of space, they never stop.
With every explosion, a burst of fun,
In this grand cosmic setup, everyone's won.

Join the laughter, it's time for a ride,
Where the universe whispers, and planets decide.
Let's revel together under the stellar show,
When witty worlds meet, the joy's on a roll!

Comet's Caper of Comedy

A comet zoomed in, tail full of glee,
Cracking wise jokes like it's meant to be.
With its fiery trail, it painted the sky,
Leaving starry-eyed chuckles as it flew by.

Meteorites threw jokes like they're hot,
As they zipped through the heavens, laughing a lot.
The celestial crowd was in stitches and tears,
Echoing laughter throughout the years.

Galactic jokes drifted in time and space,
The universe grinned, enjoying the pace.
With punchlines that sparkled and cosmic delight,
The galactic stage shone so incredibly bright.

So hitch a ride on this comet's spree,
Through the laughter of cosmos, come dance with me.
For in this great caper, joy's the rule,
And the universe's humor is no joke, it's a tool!

Comedic Constellations

In the sky, stars take their place,
Winking down with a funny face.
A giant bear spills cosmic beans,
As laughter echoes in moonlit scenes.

Planets dance in a comical spin,
Jupiter laughs as his rings wear thin.
Mars cracks jokes about his red hue,
While Venus brightens with laughter too.

Across the night, the Milky Way glows,
As comedians share their best flows.
A comet zips past, dropping a pun,
The cosmic crowd roars, 'This is fun!'

Galaxies blend in a playful spree,
Creating humor for you and me.
In this vast space, we all can find,
A universe filled with giggles entwined.

Quasar Quips

Far away, in cosmic realms,
Quasars beam; they're at the helms.
Mixing light with a splash of sass,
Cosmic comedians make time pass.

"Why did the black hole cross the void?
To put all the stars on the list denied!"
A cosmic laugh fills the event,
In the dark, funny vibes are sent.

Nebulae swirl and join the jest,
In this stellar stand-up fest.
Stars take turns to share their tales,
Giggles travel on solar gales.

With bright bursts and playful flares,
The universe buzzes with witty airs.
Quasar quips echoing in space,
Laughter floats in the emptiest place.

The Universe's Best Jokes

In the void where silence prevails,
Stars whisper jokes, where laughter sails.
"Did you hear about the cosmic cat?
It took a leap and fell flat!"

Planets chuckle, sharing their lore,
Each of them has a punchline galore.
"Why does Earth never get lost?
It knows all the paths at no cost!"

Asteroids in comical chains,
Rolling around with giggling gains.
"Why was the sun always bright?
It took shades on its cosmic flight!"

As comets streak with tails of delight,
The universe laughs late into the night.
In every corner, a joke is spun,
The cosmos smiles when we have fun.

Satellite of Satire

Orbiting round with a cheeky grin,
The satellite spins, ready to begin.
"Why does the moon never tell a lie?
Because it reflects what's nearby!"

Stars gather for the best punchlines,
Swapping stories across starry spines.
"Why was Mercury always on time?
It couldn't afford a delay; it's a crime!"

Between asteroids, laughter rings,
Joking about the strangest things.
"Why does Jupiter bring his guards?
To protect against his giant shards!"

Galactic humor fills the vast space,
Two galaxies meet and share a race.
In this cosmic tapestry we find,
A satellite of satire that's one of a kind.

Witty World of Wisps

In the galaxy's twist and spin,
Witty wisps dance with a grin.
They tickle stars, make comets laugh,
With cosmic jokes in every half.

Asteroids roll with a chuckle,
While planets burst in a chuckle.
With each orbit, a punchline flies,
In the sky where humor never dies.

Nebulas stretch, bending light,
As giggles echo, pure delight.
The universe winks in playful jest,
Where laughter reigns, it's truly blessed.

So join the fun in cosmic play,
Where each star shines in a joyful way.
In this realm where laughter swirls,
The wit of wisps forever twirls.

Comet's Comedic Tail

Comet's tail sweeps wide and bright,
With jokes that soar through the night.
A flick of humor, a dash of grace,
Sparks of laughter in endless space.

With a wink from a mighty flare,
It trails giggles across the air.
Every loop a cheeky dance,
Inviting planets for a chance.

Shooting stars shout out their puns,
As playful banter fills the runs.
In the solar wind's gentle flight,
A comet jokes with pure delight.

So catch the humor as they blaze,
In stellar paths where laughter stays.
A comedic tail in endless space,
Bringing joy to the cosmic race.

Moons and Mirth

Under the glow of a silver sphere,
Moons converse, sharing cheer.
With winks and nods, they throw the shade,
Creating laughter in cosmic parade.

Jupiter's moon cracks a smile,
While Saturn's rings spin in style.
Each orbit tells a tale of fun,
As shadows dance under the sun.

The laughter echoes through the night,
With every sparkle, pure delight.
Chasing meteors, they leap and hide,
In this frolic, no need to bide.

So spin with joy in lunar light,
Where every chuckle feels so right.
In orbits round, the mirth will flow,
As cosmic jesters steal the show.

The Celestial Comedian

In a corner of the cosmos bright,
A comedian shines, a joyful sight.
With every star, a punchline weaves,
Mirthy laughter, the heart believes.

Galactic giggles float like dust,
Where stardust sparkles, it's a must.
The universe sways to every jest,
In this special cosmic quest.

Planets spin to the rhythm of fun,
As light-years pass, the laughter runs.
With a nod to the sun's golden gleam,
The celestial bard fulfills a dream.

So gather 'round, enjoy the spree,
Under the vast expanse, wild and free.
In celestial corners, joy will spread,
A universe filled with humor's thread.

Cosmic Chortles

In the rings of gas, I make my rounds,
With jokes that orbit, laughter abounds.
Planets all listen, with ears wide and bright,
As I tell my tales in the cold, starry night.

My first punchline lands, it's a meteor's fate,
Why did the comet refuse to mate?
Because it needed space, oh what a thrill,
Makes for great laughs, all in good will.

The moons roll their eyes, they know what I mean,
Being stuck in orbits, life's not always keen.
But with a twist here and a giggle there,
We float through the cosmos, free as the air.

So join my parade, in this vast, funny sky,
With stardust and chuckles, let laughter fly.
It's a cosmic delight, a festival grand,
Where humor expands in this infinite land.

Celestial Chuckles

I joke with the stars, they twinkle in glee,
Why did the asteroid party? To feel just like me!
Inflated with humor, each galaxy spins,
While Saturn just laughs as the whole cosmos grins.

A rocket ship sauntered, looking quite sleek,
Said the space debris, "Man, I can't take a leak!"
Laughter erupts, it echoes through space,
Even black holes can't help but embrace.

Come gather, my friends, from each solar nook,
Let's whisper some jokes like an ancient old book.
And if you stumble, just float with the breeze,
For laughter's a gift, it's sure to please.

With each punchline shared, the universe grows,
In this cosmic arena, humor truly flows.
So strap in tight, for this joyride ahead,
With celestial chuckles, we'll never feel dread.

Then There Were Moons

In a galaxy far, with twinkling lights,
We gathered the moons, for laughter-filled nights.
Each one took the stage, it was quite the sight,
With comets as hecklers, we laughed with delight.

One moon cracked a joke about tides and their fuss,
"Why don't we ever take the bus?
Because we're always revolving, can't sit for a ride—
And besides, I might wax and leave you behind!"

Through this cosmic comedy, our spirits took flight,
Galaxies shimmering, oh what a night!
We shared all our tales, from craters to beams,
Turns out the void is not just for dreams.

So next time you gaze at the stars from your home,
Remember the laughter that roams through the foam.
For in every twinkle, there's humor bestowed,
And then there were moons, lighting up the road.

Cosmic Roasts

Gather 'round folks, it's the roast of the year,
Even meteors know it's time to cheer.
With nebulae grinning, and stardust to share,
We'll take potshots at planets, if you dare!

Hey Jupiter, big guy, why so full of gas?
Your storms are impressive, but look at that mass!
Your stripes might be fancy, your moons quite a bunch,
But it's your pesky rings that we all love to munch.

Mars, you think you're just spicy and red?
What's up with your selfies? Looks like you dread!
You can send all your rovers, but here's the score,
They still can't find any life on your floor.

So raise up your glasses, let laughter ignite,
In this cosmic roast, all's well and all's bright.
Let humor cascade from the stars down below,
For the cosmos is wild, and we're stealing the show!

The Puns Planet

In a realm where jokes abound,
The puns fly round and round.
A comet trips on cosmic fruit,
And laughs erupt, oh what a hoot!

Asteroids crack wise in the night,
Chortles echo in pure delight.
Black holes guffaw with a burst,
While stardust tickles, quenching thirst.

Constellations form a crew,
With every quip, their bond renews.
They share their tales, both bold and bright,
Casting giggles as they take flight.

Planets gather round to see,
Who's the funniest in this spree.
Laughter rings from Mars to beyond,
As orbits groove to comedy's song.

Stars and Stand-Up

Under the veil of cosmic jest,
Stars align for the very best.
A meteor slips on cosmic ice,
And the whole universe laughs twice.

Galactic gags and cosmic puns,
Dance with the rhythm of distant suns.
Nebulas chuckle in vibrant hues,
Lost in laughter, they can't lose.

Jokes collide like comets fly,
As laughter echoes through the sky.
A starlit stage where all can see,
Creators of joy in infinity.

With cosmic charisma, they steal the show,
Spinning tales like galaxies in tow.
Every joke a spark, illuminating the night,
In a universe where humor takes flight.

Comedic Constellations

In a sky where punchlines reign,
Constellations giggle, entertain.
Orion cracks a smile so broad,
As Cassiopeia nods, quite awed.

Pleiades spark with a witty remark,
While Ursa Major lights up the dark.
Each twinkling gem shares a fun quip,
As the Milky Way joins in the trip.

Laughter echoes in the cosmic sea,
Tickled by planets and moons with glee.
Every star a comedian, shining bright,
In the vast expanse of the velvet night.

With every joke, the cosmos sways,
As laughter ignites in endless ways.
From light-years past to future so bold,
The universe's humor forever unfolds.

Hysterical Horizons

Across horizons, humor peaks,
Where laughter blooms and mischief sneaks.
Galaxies giggle, cosmic cheer,
As every joke echoes, loud and clear.

The edge of space, a stage so grand,
Where laughter echoes through time's hand.
Light-years zoom past in funny flight,
Creating a spectacle in the night.

Horizons reach where joys unite,
In the glow of comets that dazzle bright.
A witticism spins, catches the breeze,
As astronauts chuckle in stellar ease.

The universe sways with joyous delight,
In every corner, comedy takes flight.
A cosmic carnival, laughter to share,
In horizons wide, joy fills the air.

A Witty World Within

In the silence of space, where the planets all spin,
A jester in rings has a chuckle within.
With jokes made of stardust and laughter so bright,
He tickles the comets, igniting the night.

A wink to the moons, with a twirl and a grin,
He jests at the orbits, let the fun begin!
Each quip is a meteor, racing through time,
As roars of delight echo out into rhyme.

The gravity's strong, but his humor is free,
Launching punchlines like rockets, how can this be?
With a flip of his tail, he upends the routine,
Gravity's no matter in this spaceborn scene.

In the realm of the rings where the silly reside,
Laughter's the language, come take a ride!
Where the stars burst out giggles and planets all play,
A wit-filled world beckons, come join us, hooray!

Cosmic Comedy Central

In the heart of the void, where the laughter flows tall,
A stand-up star rises, mesmerizing all.
With wisdom of eons tucked under his hat,
He spins tales of space, oh imagine that!

Planets below chuckle, they can't help but sway,
As he tickles their atmospheres, makes them okay.
His punchlines ignite like supernova's bright light,
Creating a joy that shines day and night.

From black holes he pulls, the world's quirkiest charms,
Reviewing the cosmos with laughable arms.
Asteroids listen, astounded and keen,
As he jibes with the universe, just like a machine.

With laughter as fuel and smiles like the sun,
He's got all the planets in a tizzy of fun.
So strap in your seat, for a stellar reprieve,
In this cosmic comedy, there's no room for grief!

Hilarity on High

Floating on wonders, where the laughter is light,
A jokester does pirouettes, taking flight!
With quips about gravity and truths that are bold,
Each line's a burst of brilliance, a gem to behold.

In the theater of stars, where the comets all cheer,
He pokes fun at the sun, with a wink and a sneer.
"Why do galaxies never drop by for tea?"
"Because they're busy expanding—can't you see?"

With laughter as cosmic dust, he fills every void,
Making sure the silence is thoroughly destroyed.
Nebulas giggle, and asteroids clap,
As he weaves through the cosmos like a friendly chap.

Jokes echo through chambers of bright, swirling gas,
While planets convene for a chuckle or pass.
In this high-flying act, no one's left behind,
For hilarity rules when the universe's kind!

Ringside Riddles

From the edge of the rings comes a whispering laugh,
Where each skimming particle has a punchline to craft.
A jester in motion, with stories to share,
Playing tricks on the stars, with clever flair.

"What did the comet say to the moon up above?"
"I'm passing so quick, do you feel the love?"
The answers spin slowly in the galactic din,
As planets erupt in a laugh, they all grin.

In this ringside arena, each layer's a jest,
With echoes of giggles, it's simply the best.
With humor in orbits and joy that won't fade,
He'll leave you bewildered in cosmic charades.

So gather your friends, make your way to the show,
Where the humor flows freely, and laughter will grow.
In the rings of adventure, let stories unfold,
With riddles and jests that are purest of gold!

Planetary Punchlines

Why did the planet sit so low?
It wanted some great cosmic show!
Rings of laughter, bright and round,
Jokes like meteors flying 'round.

An asteroid walked into a bar,
Stumbled over a shooting star.
'Tell me, friend, why all the fuss?'
'We just need space, come ride with us!'

Jupiter tried its hand at rhyme,
But all it got was gas and grime.
While Venus winked with glossy glee,
And said, 'Just stick with comedy!'

Neptune quipped, "I'm feeling blue,
But I can still crack a joke or two!"
Laughter echoed in the dark,
Creating joy, a cosmic spark.

The Comet's Curated Comedy

A comet streaked across the sky,
With a tail that made the stargazers sigh.
It whispered jokes with a dash of flair,
And everyone chuckled, floating in air.

Stars gathered round for the cosmic show,
What do you call a black hole with no flow?
'It's a vacuum that sucks out the fun!'
'But I'm still here, so let's get it done!'

Asteroids cheered with their rocky embrace,
Unruly satellites joined in the chase.
When meteorites roared from afar,
'At least we've got our comedy star!'

Each punchline shone like a galaxy new,
Filling the void with laughter's debut.
In the dance of the cosmos so vast,
The joy of the universe was unsurpassed.

Giggles in the Galaxy

In the Milky Way, the giggles abound,
A supernova joke just astounds.
'Your face looks like it's lost its glow!'
'Guess I'm just waiting for my show!'

Planets play games of cosmic charades,
Spinning tales with winks and parades.
Mars cracked a smile, 'What's in a name?
I'm known for my reds, but it's all just a game!'

Black holes spinning with a twist of fate,
'Why'd the light lose its date?'
'Because it saw the pull of my charm!'
Laughter erupted, good times on the farm.

Each galaxy bursts with quirky delight,
Where laughter shines in the endless night.
So if you look up and see a glow,
It's just the universe, ready to show!

Wit in the Wilderness of Space

In the vastness of space, comedy reigns,
As stars spin around with clever refrains.
'What did the sun say to the moon?'
'You're out too late, it's afternoon!'

Galaxies wobble with guffaws and cheer,
A pulsar's punchline, oh so sincere.
Satellites danced with their shiny bling,
Twirling around, making laughter spring.

A rogue planet joked, 'I'm lost, what's the deal?'
'I'll map out the stars; together we'll feel!'
Humor weaves through the fabric of space,
Turning frowns into smiles, a celestial embrace.

With each cosmic giggle, the darkness recedes,
In the wilderness where laughter leads.
So embrace the stars and let joy ignite,
In the universe's wild comedic light!

Cosmic Comedy Hour

In the void where stars collide,
A punchline travels far and wide.
With comets tailing humor's flight,
The cosmos bursts with laughter bright.

In black holes where no jokes escape,
The universe grooves in cosmic shape.
Planets spin with a chuckle's grace,
As asteroids join this wild space race.

The moons all share a witty jest,
While nebulae give their best guest.
Each tick of time, a giggle shared,
In the expanse, all souls are bared.

So come gather 'round this stellar show,
Where humor's spark begins to glow.
With every laugh, the night will bend,
In this vast sky, let's all pretend.

Rings of Laughter

Around a giant, swirling jest,
Rings of laughter put to the test.
Each giggle dances in the air,
Echoing tales of cosmic flair.

A comet zips with snickers loud,
While meteors crash but still feel proud.
The gravity pulls a funny bone,
While stardust sparkles, laughter's throne.

The moons take turns to crack a smile,
As space-time twists in humorous style.
With every wobble, humor's found,
Spinning in circles, cosmic sound.

With each orbit, a tale unfolds,
As space laughs hard through eons old.
In the night sky, a jest awaits,
Bringing glee to the starlit states.

Galactic Giggles

Through cosmic seas, the laughter flows,
With every star, a whimsy glows.
Black holes tease with a sassy wink,
While all the planets stop to think.

Shooting stars play tag at night,
While asteroids share their cosmic bite.
In a galaxy where joy ignites,
The universe beams with playful sights.

With space-time ripples, jokers blend,
Bantering like there's no end.
The solar winds crack a grin,
As laughter echoes from within.

So here we float, all merry and bold,
In this space where fun is gold.
Join the dance of the stellar crowd,
Galactic giggles ringing loud.

The Jester of the Planets

In the court of stars, a jester reigns,
With jokes that sidestep all the pains.
Laughing moons and stars aglow,
In this comical cosmic show.

A bounce from orbit, a twist and spin,
Where even comets can crack a grin.
The rings of gas, they swirl and twirl,
As laughter makes the whole sky whirl.

With a wink and nod, the jester is bold,
Tales of old that never get old.
As planets giggle and take their place,
In the grand scheme of cosmic grace.

So gather round, in this stellar site,
Enjoy the jest on this starry night.
For in the space where laughter swoops,
The jester's joy proudly loops.

Cosmic Observations & Punchlines

In a galaxy not so far,
Stars twinkle like they're at the bar.
Asteroids roll, making a fuss,
While comets joke on the cosmic bus.

Planets spin with a dizzy cheer,
Jupiter's jokes pull in the sphere.
Mars cracks up, and Earth joins in,
While Venus winks with a cheeky grin.

The Milky Way laughs in a swirl,
As black holes chuckle, giving a whirl.
Supernovae burst with a big punch,
And starlight giggles, oh what a bunch!

Galaxies gather, sharing their jest,
In the vastness of space, they're all dressed best.
Light-years away, the humor unfolds,
In the cosmos, laughter never gets old.

Constellation Chronicles

Orion tells tales of his brave fight,
While Ursa Major brings the night light.
Scorpio's sting is a ticklish tease,
His laughter echoes with cosmic ease.

Andromeda rolls her eyes with flair,
As Cassiopeia combs her hair.
The stars dance in a sly parade,
While comets slip into the charade.

Little Dipper spouts puns so bright,
Shooting stars laugh and take flight.
Pegasus gallops across the dark,
And black holes whisper a cheeky spark.

In the vast expanse, humor flows free,
As constellations giggle in glee.
With each twinkle, a punchline unfurls,
In the astral sea of twinkling pearls.

Mirthful Moons

Full moon beams with a radiant smile,
While waning gibbous goes the extra mile.
Crescent giggles, waxing cheeky bright,
As new moons plot their return to light.

Luna jests with a playful wink,
While shadows dance, and stardust drinks.
The tides cackle, riding the waves,
As craters chuckle in lunar caves.

Eclipses come for a surprise show,
Blocking the sun in a comical flow.
Moons of Mars are snickering late,
While Phobos claims it's a cosmic fate.

With every phase, a prankster's game,
Moonbeams twirl in their heavenly frame.
A mirthful night beneath cosmic blooms,
We laugh along with the blissful moons.

Heavenly Humor

Celestial giggles erupt from the stars,
As they bounce jokes off of Mars.
The universe grins with a twinkling glee,
And asteroids laugh, rolling wild and free.

A supernova starts a spontaneous jest,
While the universe hosts its comedy fest.
Nebulae cloak in a shimmering guise,
Telling tales that tickle the skies.

Quasars roar with laughter loud,
While Saturn spins, and the starlings crowd.
The cosmos sways in a comic embrace,
As every planet joins the race.

Galactic chuckles echo through night,
With each twinkling star, it feels so right.
Amid the stars, we share the fun,
In the heavenly realm, laughter's never done.

Nebula of Nonsense

In a cloud of gas and dust,
Stars are playing hide-and-seek,
One laughed, 'I need a gust!'
'I'd fly high, but I'm too weak.'

Comets zoom with silly grins,
While asteroids roll in a laugh,
'Look at my rock-hard chins!'
'Hope you enjoy my goofy staff!'

The Milky Way joins in the fun,
For it spins like a corkscrew toy,
Nebulas join, one by one,
Creating chaos, oh what joy!

A supernova burst leads to cheer,
'What a bang!' they all exclaim,
'Let's toast to another year!'
In this sky, nothing's the same.

Planetary Puns and Jibes

Jupiter jumps with a wacky boom,
'Satellites, don't trip on my shoelace!'
Mars chimes in, 'Not in this room,
I've got the best dinner space!'

On Mercury, jokes fly fast,
'Why did the planet get in a fight?'
The quick reply is never last,
'It couldn't handle the heat tonight!'

Venus spins with comedic flair,
'What did Earth say to the moon?'
'You're so full, you great big pair,
Hurry up, or I'll call a loony tune!'

Uranus giggles, finding his groove,
'Why did the star bring a straw?'
'To sip on the light and move,
While I watch the cosmos in awe!'

Titan's Tumultuous Tales

Titan tells tales of cosmic fun,
'Once I danced with a comet's tail!'
Gravity said, 'You'll weigh a ton!'
But we laughed, we couldn't fail!'

With aliens joined in the right spot,
They joked about the best moon pies,
'In space, we're piping hot,
But inside, we're all just shy!'

'What's the matter?' said a bright star,
'Tell me why all the fuss and prattle?'
'Just trying to reach that bar,
But we're stuck in this cosmic cattle!'

With each story, the laughter grew,
'These adventures we won't forget!'
All around, the cosmos flew,
In Titan's tales, they're truly set.

Space-Time Shenanigans

Through spacetime, the giggles swirled,
Time travelers with laughs to share,
'Did you hear how the galaxies twirled?
They got dizzy in the cosmic air!'

Backwards laughter, oh what a sight,
Einstein cracks a pun, what a schemer,
'Let's make rhymes about this plight,
And shine brighter, like a dreamer!'

Black holes pull in all the fun,
'What's the secret to your flight?'
'Just contain it in a bun,
Then launch it with all your might!'

As stars gather for a final cheer,
They know it's all just a jest,
In this union, there's nothing to fear,
For fun in space is always the best!

www.ingramcontent.com/pod-product-compliance
Lightning Source LLC
Chambersburg PA
CBHW071835160426
43209CB00003B/315